THE Aspiring Artist's STUDIO

Contemporary Mosaics

THE
Aspiring Artist's
STUDIO

Contemporary
Mosaics

Ronit Attias

Sterling Publishing Co., Inc.
New York

Designed by Eddie Goldfine
Layout by Ariane Rybski
Edited by Shoshana Brickman
Photography by Matt Cohen

Blaine Harrington III/Corbis 11
James Sparshatt/Corbis 17
Elan Penn 9, 13, 14, 15

Library of Congress Cataloging-in-Publication Data Available

2   4   6   8   10   9   7   5   3   1

Published by Sterling Publishing Co., Inc.
387 Park Avenue South, New York, NY 10016
© 2007 by Penn Publishing Ltd.
Distributed in Canada by Sterling Publishing
c/o Canadian Manda Group, 165 Dufferin Street,
Toronto, Ontario, Canada M6K 3H6
Distributed in the United Kingdom by GMC Distribution Services,
Castle Place, 166 High Street, Lewes, East Sussex, England BN7 1XU
Distributed in Australia by Capricorn Link (Australia) Pty. Ltd.
P.O. Box 704, Windsor, NSW 2756, Australia

Sterling ISBN-13: 978-1-4027-3257-7
ISBN-10: 1-4027-3257-0

For information about custom editions, special sales, premium and
corporate purchases, please contact Sterling Special Sales
Department at 800-805-5489 or specialsales@sterlingpub.com.

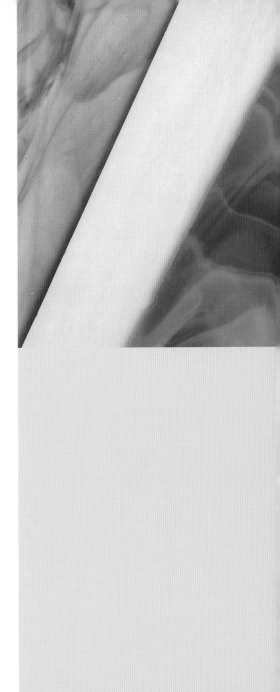

About This Book

This book is a compilation of mosaic works by Ronit Attias, a leading artist in the field of contemporary mosaic. The works were completed over a span of several years, and using a variety of materials. They vary in size and dimension, ranging from 60-inch sculptures to tabletop lamps, from expansive murals to decorative candlesticks.

The design process for many of these projects involved computer sketching. A description of this process and a selection of computer images are included, giving readers a sense of how valuable this technology can be in the field of contemporary mosaic.

An introduction to the history of mosaic opens the book. After this is an explanation of how the art evolved over time, incorporating new materials and elements, and emerging as a contemporary form of art. This is followed by vibrant full color photographs and descriptions of more than thirty projects, several of which are accompanied by step-by-step photographs, computer images, and instructions.

Readers who are familiar with mosaic art will be able to adapt these projects to suit various surfaces, sizes, and materials. Readers who are new to the field will find a festival of colors within the pages of the book, a small gallery they can flip through at leisure for inspiration and ideas. Every reader will be enchanted by the range of possibilities available to the contemporary mosaic artist, and delighted by the remarkable and distinct results.

Enjoy your reading!

History of Mosaic

Mosaic is an ancient art that has enthralled artists for thousands of years. It has evolved over time, maintaining its essential elements while embracing new forms and materials, blossoming into an eminently contemporary form of art. Mosaic is a puzzle that involves the compilation of innumerable tesserae into a unified whole, a new entity that is completely original. A mosaic work has an energy that is greater than the sum of its parts, due to the distinct power of every piece and the unique assembly of the pieces together.

The history of mosaic spans thousands of years, and early mosaics composed of shells and clay have been found dating to the fourth millennium BCE. By the third century BCE, mosaic was an established art in ancient Greece, and mosaic floors depicting mythological figures and traditional stories were installed in the homes of wealthy and influential citizens. Early mosaics were made from small pebbles; later ones included marble and glass as well. They were designed and laid by craftspeople who passed their skills down from generation to generation.

The Romans developed the art of mosaic further, expanding it to areas such as theatres, public baths, markets, and private homes. During this period, mosaic carpets made a small migration, moving from floors to decorate walls as well. The Romans increased their palette of materials to include slate, limestone, glass, and marble. Dominant themes during this period include mythological figures, well-known tales, and vivid underwater scenes. Remains of these mosaics can be seen today in several places, including France, Turkey, Cyprus, Tunisia, and Morocco.

The Euthymius Monastery, Judean Desert, Israel

The dominant type of the mosaic design is geometric combinations in different versions.

With the spread of Christianity, mosaic art spread as well, and became enriched with new themes and materials. Massive, vibrant mosaic pieces were installed on church floors, walls, and vaults. New techniques evolved, including the development of tesserae with rough, irregular surfaces, allowing artists to play with light according to the orientation of the pieces. New materials used during this period include colored glass and precious gold and silver leaf.

For the next several hundred years, mosaic was used to decorate churches throughout the Mediterranean region. Splendid works dating from the Byzantine period onward represent biblical figures and tales with remarkable realism and beauty. These mosaics fulfilled an important didactic function as well, as they allowed biblical stories to be conveyed visually to people who were, for the most part, illiterate.

At the same time, Moslem artists used mosaics to beautify mosques. These magnificent pieces differed from Christian mosaics as they did not portray human figures. Richly decorated with animals, plants, and flowers, they often included remarkably intricate geometric designs. Mosaics from this period can be viewed in several countries, including Israel, Syria, Libya, and Spain.

Mosaic art declined for a period, then underwent a dramatic transformation in the early twentieth century. This revival occurred thanks to innovative artists such as Antoni Gaudí, who went beyond entrenched ideas of art and architecture, and began combining materials and mediums into a wholly modern form of mosaic.

(continued on page 12)

Triumph of Venus

Floor mosaic at Amphitrite House,
Bulla Regia, Tunisia

Together, Gaudí and Josep Maria Jujol created Parc Güell in Barcelona, a wonderland of brilliant mosaic sculptures and buildings. Originally contracted to be a cluster of private homes, Parc Güell is now one of the world's most beautiful parks.

Another major figure in the field of contemporary mosaic art is Niki de Saint Phalle, the French artist who broke boundaries in various fields, including sculpting, painting, and mosaic. After visiting Parc Güell, de Saint Phalle was inspired to create a sculpture park from the perspective of a woman. Located in Tuscany, the park is known as Giardino dei Tarocchi, or the Tarot Garden.

Contemporary mosaic follows in the tradition of its ancient and modern predecessors, with artists incorporating their own adaptations and innovations. While some principles remain the same, other elements are always changing, depending upon the experience, inspiration, and courage of the artist. It is an immensely adaptable and rich art open to every possibility within the artist's imagination.

Herod's Western Palace, Masada, Israel

Magnificient, richly colored mosaic pavement with circles and border ornaments of plant and geometric designs. This room may have been King Herod's throne room, the seat of authority when he was in residence at Masada.

Elements in Contemporary Mosaic

Subject

During Greek and Roman times, mosaics often told stories from mythological and legendary sources. As the Church began to embrace the art, religious stories and themes became dominant subjects in the field. Today, mosaics may incorporate any subject or theme at all. While they may still include biblical stories and legends, they can also relate to any other issue under the sun—including the sun itself. Mosaic can be used to make figurative or abstract portraits, playful or serious sculptures, functional or primarily aesthetic objects.

Location

Mosaics were once limited to commissions by wealthy or influential individuals or authorities. Only noblemen, rulers, and other people with vast resources could afford to hire the skilled laborers required to work for days, months, even years on a mosaic floor or wall. Due to the high costs, mosaics were rarely seen in private homes or public places. Today, mosaics may be found any place people have felt a desire to add beauty. Often included in elegant buildings and fine homes, they are also found in subway systems, public parks, airports, office buildings, and private homes. Still an art of fine craftsmanship and beauty, mosaics can now be found in diverse locations, allowing more people to enjoy their distinct and unique beauty.

Indeed, one of my favorite mosaics is the IMAGINE mosaic located in New York City's

(continued on page 16)

Tiling at Dome of the Rock,
Jerusalem, Israel

*The most lavish mosaics to survive from ancient or medieval
times anywhere.*

Central Park. This piece, created in memory of
John Lennon and situated in the park's
Strawberry Fields, is a source of inspiration,
reflection, and contemplation for me, as well
as for millions of park visitors. This mosaic is a
reminder of all the dreams described in that
famous song, the hope for peace and sharing, an
end to greed and hunger. These eternal wishes,
and this internationally known contemporary
song, are evoked in this timeless piece of mosaic
art. The inspiration behind the design is an
ancient mosaic floor found in the ruins of
Pompeii. Just as the dream for peace is eternal, so
is the style of this mosaic. Made from black and
white rocks, the colors are as basic as the
universal hope for peace. The piece demonstrates
how contemporary mosaic combines the old and
the new, integrating the timeless message of a
modern song into a classic design that was
preserved in an ancient mosaic.

Mosaic Objects

Initially, mosaics were situated only on floors.
After several hundred years, mosaic objects
shifted to include walls as well, but the basic
style—flat and one-dimensional—remained the
same. Today, mosaic may be placed on almost any
item. It may be laid flat on a floor or molded to
fit around a sculpture; it may surround a mirror
or decorate a statue; it may border a window or
be incorporated into a desk. Mosaic tesserae can
be incorporated into jewelry, sculptures, chairs,
candlesticks, and clocks. Functional items
enhanced with mosaic retain their functionality
while fulfilling an aesthetic element as well.

(continued on page 18)

Spires on Church of the Sagrada Familia

*Tilework mosaic covers the spires on the Church of the Sagrada
Familia in Barcelona.
Designed by Antonio Gaudi y Cornet*

Combination of Materials

The first mosaics were made from shells, pebbles, and other natural materials that were inset in earthen floors. Over time, techniques were developed for breaking stone and marble, and for making glazed and glass tesserae. While all of these materials remain vital to the contemporary artist, a range of other options also exists that is vast and varying, open to the artist's needs and imagination. The base may be made from any solid material, including wood, iron, stainless steel, or concrete. The tesserae may be any material the artist feels appropriate, including glass, marble, mirror, or ceramic tile. The diversity of materials allows mosaics to come alive, bestowing them with the ability to incur feelings and emotions. The materials used in mosaic are intimately related to the subject; just as the subject has no limits, neither does the range of materials used in its rendering.

About the Author

Author and artist Ronit Attias transforms the ancient art of mosaic into a contemporary art. Ronit combines materials, contrasts colors, and mixes mediums to integrate mosaic into a wide variety of objects. Using a combination of traditional and modern materials, she creates mosaic art that is both functional and aesthetic. It includes large works such as sculptures, murals, and tables, as well as home accessories including candlesticks, lamps and small clocks, and jewelry.

Ronit graduated from Escola Superior de Disseny I d'Art Llotja and Escola Massana Centre d'Art I Disseny, both located in Barcelona and considered among the world's top centers for mosaic learning. Ronit participated in art exhibitions at the Musées Royaux d'Art et d'Histoire and the Musée du Tram.

Ronit's use of computer sketching and the integration of both modern and traditional motifs result in pieces that are vibrant, original, and contemporary.

The creative process in every piece of art begins with inspiration. It may come from something personal, such as an experience, a feeling, a color, or a cherished object. It may come from people I know or happen to meet, from casual conversations, from a book or a movie, from dreams or memories. Inspiration may also come from size or color requirements, or a specific request from a client.

When transferring inspiration into a mosaic work, one creates a feeling, an emotion that extends beyond the piece. This requires passion, and no mosaic piece is complete without the personal involvement of the artist.

Another essential element, required in every stage of the process, is patience. Patience, patience, and more patience. Much as in life, one gains understanding as one works on a project and certain elements can be determined only as one works. Just as patience is important in life, it is also critical in the creative process of mosaic art. The final product is like a puzzle with all of its parts; it is the result of both passion and patience working in tandem.

The next stage involves practical considerations such as where the object will be situated, its size, the materials that will be used for its base, and the colors and types of tesserae.

Almost any solid surface can serve as the base for mosaic. Mosaics that are installed outdoors require a base that can withstand the elements. For example, a set of garden tables for a hotel, the floor of a swimming pool, or a mosaic statue to be situated in a public park, must all be able to withstand rain, snow, subzero temperatures, intense heat, and direct sunlight. Iron, cement, and stainless steel are all weather-resistant materials that can be used for such projects.

Once the base has been chosen, decisions about the tesserae are considered. The essence of mosaic is the tesserae, the individual pieces of tile, glass, or rock that are combined to create a new whole. Tesserae come in a multitude of colors, styles, and materials. Although firm objects by nature, tesserae become extremely flexible when incorporated into mosaic. They are transformed according to their location, cut, and position. The angle of light, the contrast with other pieces, the size and the shape of the pieces and of the mosaic object—all of these elements affect the final appearance and character of the work.

Issues such as texture, intensity of color, contrast of the colors, placement of the pieces, and sense of movement are all considered when selecting tesserae. A rounded, natural-hued pebble may convey the warmth and earthiness suited to a garden path; rough-edged vibrant orange smalti may convey the heat and intensity innate in a blazing sun. Each tessera is affected by where it is situated, what other tesserae surround it, the color of the grout, and the size of the project. Each piece has its own energy and a successful mosaic channels all of these energies, combining them in a matter that is harmonious, even if it is unconventional. The variables—and the potential—are endless.

The mosaic process begins with a dream or idea. It ends with a tangible object that may be functional on a practical level, for its ability to serve as a table, mirror, or clock, or for its ability to stir feelings of happiness, warmth, vibrancy, life. Between these two stages there is another stage in my creative process—computer sketching—that allows me to bridge the gap between intangible ideas and concrete objects.

Computer Sketching

The computer is a vital tool in my work. It is the pencil with which I draw and the paint with which I add color. It enables me to produce images in two or three dimensions, allowing me to advance the planning of my mosaic work by making digital adjustments to color, size, and shape. Despite being time-intensive, computer sketching is an asset to me, as the artist, and to my clients.

Computer sketching comprises an important step in the planning process. It opens a window into my imagination, allowing my vision to become almost tangible to my clients, and enabling the mosaic work to be visible long before the first tesserae has been placed.

Of course, the final product is always more impressive than the digital image. Furthermore, it is never identical to what is projected on the computer screen, since the impact of mosaic art goes far beyond the visual. Still, the benefits afforded by this technology are great, as it allows us to obtain an idea of how the final project will look. Ultimately, this results in fewer surprises at the end.

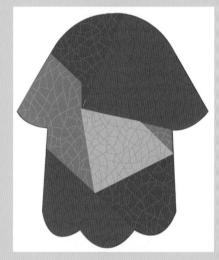

In the first stage, I transfer the vision from my mind to the computer screen. I hone my thoughts with the curser, making adjustments to size, color, and composition. When this step is complete, I show the client my initial conception of the project.

After clients have viewed the digital image, we discuss their responses. If changes are necessary, we try out different colors or shapes. We make adjustments during the planning stages of the project, working together until we have an image that fulfills their needs.

Computer sketching significantly reduces the gap between the artist's vision and the client's expectations. In a sense, it articulates the mosaic fantasy in a language that can be understood by people who have little experience in the field.

Materials and Tools

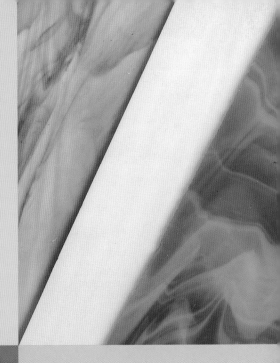

The range of materials that can be used to make mosaics is almost limitless. As for tools, a number of basic items are critical for every artist. Both materials and tools can be found in art supply shops or on the Internet.

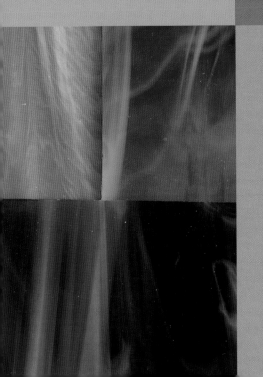

Materials

Base material

Almost any sturdy material can be used as a base for contemporary mosaic. My choice of material is based on a number of considerations, including color, weight, and durability. Clearly, mosaics that will be situated outdoors require a base that is durable and weather-resistant. For such pieces, materials such as iron, rock, aluminum, and cement are ideal. Indoor mosaics may be based on any of these materials, as well as less resilient materials such as wood or plaster. Each base material has its own characteristics and energies which affect the overall feeling of the mosaic.

Tesserae

The general term for the pieces which form a mosaic design is tesserae (tessera in singular), from the Greek for "cubes of marble". In contemporary mosaic, the options for tesserae have gone far beyond marble cubes, and include virtually any material that the artist wishes to incorporate. Of course, the lifespan of the mosaic relates to the durability of its tesserae. In my work, I generally use the following types of tesserae:

Ceramic tiles come in a variety of textures, colors, and styles. They may be glazed or unglazed, thin or thick, patterned or solidly painted. Ceramic tiles are highly accessible, and are made using a variety of processes. Ceramic tiles present an excellent opportunity for recycling in mosaic art, as used ceramics can be brought back to life in mosaic art.

Ceramic tiles

Colored glass comes in a limitless variety of colors, and a single sheet may be a solid color or be streaked with several brilliant shades and hues. Colored glass is broken into small pieces using wheeled glass cutters or tile cutters. Colored glass has a smooth texture that is pleasant to touch.

Gold and silver leaf tesserae are among the most cherished materials for mosaic work. Made by sandwiching a thin sheet of 24 karat gold or sterling silver between two layers of glass, they are handmade following a centuries-old Venetian tradition. Tesserae made with precious metals convey a sense of grandeur, royalty, and presence. Integrating them into contemporary mosaic adds a regal touch, an unrivaled sense of splendor and elegance.

 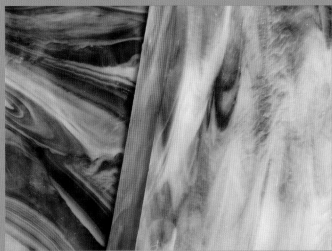

Colored glass

Gold and silver leaf tesserae

Marble and other natural stones are one of the most ancient sources for mosaic tesserae. They come in a natural palette of colors and may have either polished or unpolished finishes. Marble is excellent for creating outdoor mosaics, as it is very durable.

Mirrors add a surprising, ever-changing dimension to mosaic. They reflect whatever faces them, creating an intrinsic relationship between the mosaic and its surroundings. Mirrors are also fun. Adding mirror tiles to any project alters its mood, creating a dimension that is unpredictable, interactive, and entertaining.

Marble and other natural stones

Smalti is considered one of the finest materials for making mosaic. Vibrantly colored glass cut into small, irregularly shaped pieces, smalti is prized for its wide range of colors and refractive surface. Manufactured in small batches, each smalti tessera is distinct due to its shape, the way in which it refracts light, and the presence of interior bubbles.

Vitreous glass tiles come in a variety of colors and may be flecked with gold or other metallic powders. Vitreous glass is durable and smooth, suitable for floors, walls, tabletops, and any other flat surfaces. The tiles may be used whole or broken into smaller pieces using tile nippers.

Adhesives and grout

Choosing the right adhesive is crucial in securing the longevity of a mosaic work.

Epoxy adhesive is a resin-based, two-part adhesive used for gluing tesserae to plastic, wood, or metal. It is suitable for both indoor and outdoor mosaics.

Plastic adhesive is often used for projects that will be installed indoors. It can be used to glue ceramic pieces and vitreous glass to wood or nylon mesh.

Grout comes in a variety of colors. It can be colored manually or purchased in a range of pre-mixed colors. Grout is not necessary in all projects; when used effectively, it can emphasize color either through contrast or similarity.

Smalti

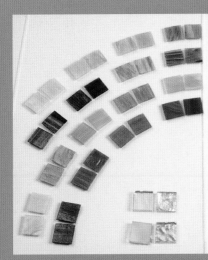

Vitreous glass

Tools

Brush for applying grout.

Cotton cloth for cleaning excess grout off mosaic.

Glass grinder for smoothing edges of cut pieces of glass. This is particularly important when working on figurative or symmetrical items.

Glue gun for applying epoxy adhesive to base materials.

Goggles for protecting the eyes from glass slivers and other harmful materials.

Hammer for breaking ceramic tiles into smaller pieces.

Mat knife for cutting nylon mesh and other materials.

Nylon mesh for providing an intermediary mosaic base until a project is laid in its permanent location.

Round-nose pliers in various sizes for picking up small tesserae and bending wires.

Scissors for cutting nylon mesh and other materials.

Spreaders for mixing and applying grout.

Tile nippers for nipping glass and ceramic tiles. This is one of the most important tools in my workshop.

Tweezers for grasping particularly small pieces of tesserae and positioning them with precision and accuracy.

Wheeled glass cutter for scoring and cutting colored glass.

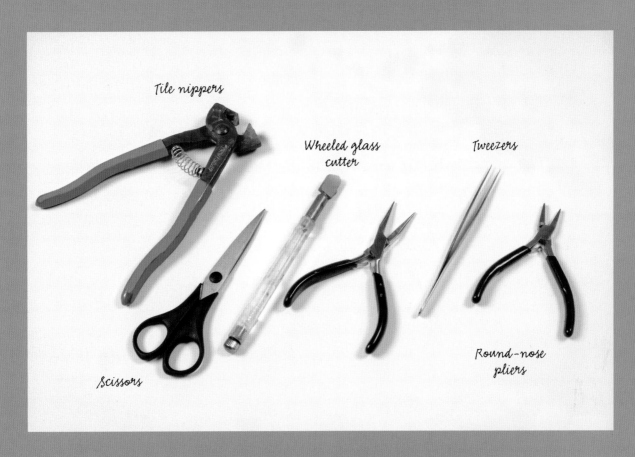

Tile nippers

Wheeled glass
cutter

Tweezers

Scissors

Round-nose
pliers

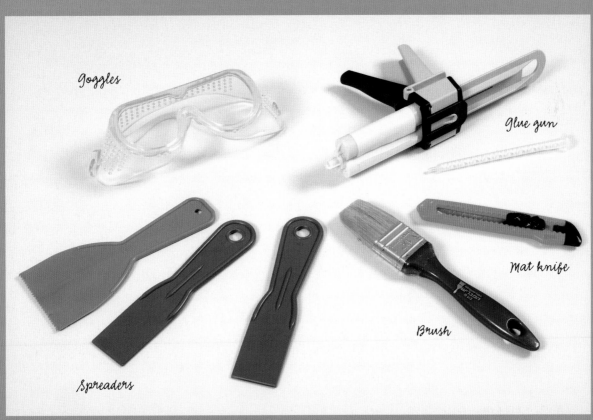

Goggles

Glue gun

Mat knife

Spreaders

Brush

sculptures

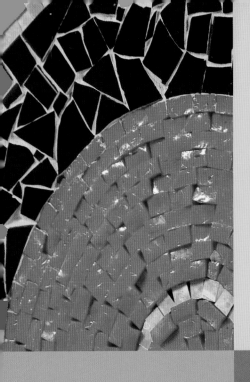

Some of the sculptures in this chapter are suited for an outdoor park or boulevard; others are perfect for an office or living room. All of these pieces enhance the environments in which they are situated, adding color, joy, and vivacity.

Sculptures

Look around most modern environments, from hospitals to universities, from banks to airports, and you'll notice an abundance of sculptures. Small or large, stationary or kinetic, abstract or figurative, playful or historic, modern or traditional, sculptures are one of the most important types of art; increasingly they are being included into every environment that people visit and inhabit. Durable sculptures may be situated in outdoor parks or subway stations; more delicate pieces may be found in museums, private homes, and fine shops. Sculptures grace the entrances of modern skyscrapers, are installed in public buildings and along major boulevards, decorate private gardens and adorn commercial shopping centers. They are located in every place that people pass their time, whether for work or leisure.

The value of a sculpture lies in its existence. Sculptures have power and energy; they affect how people feel and function. Recent studies show sculptures in hospitals can actually help people recuperate and heal by making them feel happy, lively, and optimistic. Sculptures also contribute to the well-being of people who work in hospitals—doctors, nurses, clerks, and volunteers—by bringing permanent rays of light into a work environment that is often difficult and distressing. Clearly, if hospital workers benefit from having sculptures in their midst, employees who work in less stressful environments also get a boost from sculptures.

Sculptures convey their energy through a number of elements, including size, color, and texture. A brightly colored flower can bring a sense of springtime indoors in the middle of winter; a vibrant sun will brighten up a room even on the darkest night. Unlike many pieces of art, sculptures have a sensory element as well—they can be touched. In mosaic sculptures, the texture of the tesserae and the base material both contribute to the sculpture's effect and presence. The complete impact is multifaceted; it starts with the eye, extends to the touch, and includes the subconscious effect of size, shape, and color.

A sculpture may evoke an abstract image or a realistic figure; it may conjure an element of history, fantasy, or legend. Sculptures influence the context in which they are situated; a colorful sculpture may enliven a sleek modern building; a playful sculpture in a park may cause visitors to laugh, giggle, reminisce, or dream. A sculpture in a bank adds a sense of wealth and security; in a city center, it may recall a historic moment.

Sculptures that are in harmony with their surroundings add a positive energy that completes the environment. Thus the function of a sculpture is in its existence: to add beauty, conjure feelings, affect people.

Flower of Love

This magnificent flower has two distinct faces made with complementary compositions and colors. The base is wrought iron; the mosaic is comprised of ceramic tiles, smalti, and 24 karat gold leaf tesserae. The gold leaf tesserae, formed by making a sandwich of a thin sheet of gold between two squares of glass, contributes to the richness and luxury of the piece. It is ideal for an executive office, airport lounge, or elegant boutique.

Materials

Wrought iron base

Black paint

Epoxy adhesive

Black, red, burgundy, white ceramic tiles

Red smalti

24 karat gold leaf tesserae

Gray grout

Directions

The first stage in the process involved drawing preliminary sketches on the computer. It was during this stage that I decided on the shapes of the flower's various components: a wide round face, heart-shaped leaves, and a stem that bends gently and gracefully.

I adjusted the dimensions of the various elements until I was pleased with the overall composition. In its full size, it stands 60 inches tall and has a width of 30 inches. Of course, the statue can be made in any size, as long as the relative proportions of each component stay the same.

The next stage involved choosing the base material. I decided upon wrought iron, so that the statue would be durable and solid. Each of the parts was formed separately then welded into place. A 2-inch rim along the edge of the flower

preliminary computer sketch

Materials

provides a border to support the tesserae. The iron base was galvanized, painted black, and cured in a paint finishing oven.

Different designs for each face, both of which convey a sense of opulence and richness, were sketched on the computer. I altered the colors as I laid the mosaic, resulting in a final effect that is similar but much more powerful than the initial design.

The ceramic tiles were nipped into various shapes. In particular, I used many triangular pieces of tile, as they contrast nicely with the rectangular shape of the smalti and the round shape of the flower.

An epoxy adhesive was used and the tesserae were laid in sections. The adhesive was allowed to dry completely, then gray grout was applied to the areas covered with ceramic tiles. All of the other areas were left grout-free.

Flower of Love, full view, one side

 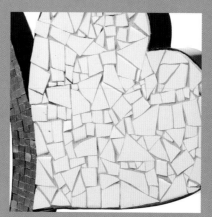 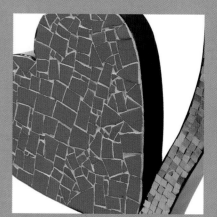

Flower of Love, sectional close-ups

Flower of Love, full view, one side

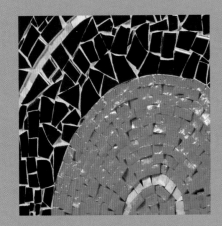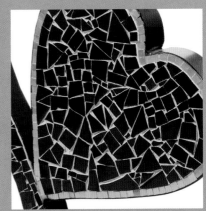

Flower of Love, sectional close-ups

Sunflower

In French, it is tournesol; *in Spanish, it is* girasol; *in Arabic, it is* abed el sams—*all of these names describe the sunflower's most basic instinct—to shift position as it follows the daily progression of the sun.*

This sculpture brings the sun with it wherever it is situated, in every season and any location. Made of silver-painted wrought iron, one side is set with brown smalti and pieces of yellow and green colored glass. The other side includes various shades of orange and yellow smalti, shades of green colored glass, and bronze tesserae. The statue stands 60 inches high.

Marguerite

This daisy is made of ceramic tiles, smalti, and mirrors laid on wrought iron painted red. Different colors and diverse compositions are used on either side. One face is white ceramic and smalti, with circles of red and yellow smalti. Mirrors and red ceramic are used to make the stem. The other face features blue and red ceramic tiles and bright yellow smalti. The composition on both sides is happy and joyful.

Tulip

Tulips are noble, sleek, and exquisitely simple. The mosaic version of this dignified flower is made of gold-painted wrought iron, and laid with various shades of yellow and green ceramic tiles. The same colors are featured on both faces of the flower, in different compositions. This technique, which creates two totally distinct faces, demonstrates how every facet in a mosaic piece contributes to its final effect. That is, the energy of the final piece is not just a result of the size, shape, and color of the statue, but is also formed by the shape of the tesserae, the composition of the colors, and the flow of the pieces.

Tulip, full view, four perspectives

Heart Flower

Love is one of the most natural feelings in the world. It is also the most
important emotion, the one that makes the world go round. This flower is a
unique botanic creation, inspired by my love of flowers, and my love of love.
People who see it often marvel that such a flower doesn't bloom naturally.

The base is wrought iron painted green. The mosaic composition on both
sides contains orange and green ceramic tiles and mirrors. The mirrors reflect
the nature of love, an emotion that is mutual and interactive, that causes
one to act and react. One looks at this piece and becomes a part of it, just as
one becomes a part of love as soon as one feels love. The mirrors create a
feeling of give-and-take, connection, and relationship.

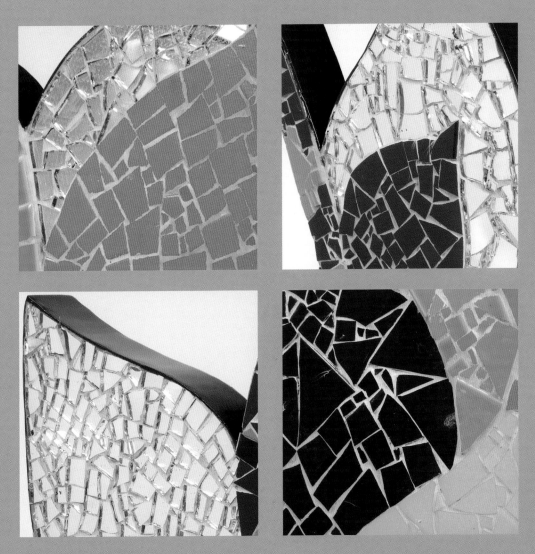

Heart Flower, sectional close-ups

Mosaic Time

This radiant wall sculpture shines all day and all year. Never dimmed by nightfall or clouds, it brings permanent warmth to any home, office, or lobby. The base is wrought iron; the face is composed of vivid red, orange, and yellow smalti, as well as various shades of colored glass and bronze tesserae.

The piece was inspired by the sun I so deeply missed while living in Europe for eight years. In fact, a chronic lack of sunshine was a major element in my decision to return to Israel. Like plants, people yearn for the sun's warm rays to grow and develop. Just as the sun brings sweetness to seasonal fruits, it sweetens people's lives as well, giving us warmth and comfort, inspiration and vivacity.

Practically speaking, the sun is also a measure of our lives. It may determine when we rise and what we do throughout the day. It determines how much light we have in a day and in a season. With these considerations, it only seemed natural to add a clock to this sculpture, giving it a function that reflects its nature. This sun has a 43-inch radius and a depth of 2 inches. Smaller wall clocks inspired by this piece can be seen on page 113.

Preliminary computer sketch

Sectional close-up

Mosaic Time, full view

Small Tulip

*This sculpture is bright and happy, light and colorful. The base
is wrought iron, and the faces on each side are different. On
one side, the flower is composed of deep purple and orange
colored glass and the stem is made from mirror. On the other
side, the flower is composed of orange colored glass and the stem
is made from dark green colored glass.*

Small Tulip, full view

This sculpture stands 24 inches high and can be installed to be either kinetic or stationary. The kinetic option allows one to spin the sculpture gently in the base, thereby changing the orientation of the face.

Forever Yours, red face

This statue is a perfect way to say "I Love You". Bright and vibrant, one face is made with red colored glass and 24 karat gold leaf tesserae. The border of gold on this face, and the pieces of gold interspersed in the stem, give it a truly romantic, passionate look. The other side features black and white colored glass tesserae, with a border of silver leaf tesserae. This side has a look that is both classic and contemporary.

Forever Yours, black face

This sculpture stands 24 inches high and can be installed to be either kinetic or stationary. The kinetic option allows one to spin the sculpture gently in the base, thereby changing the orientation of the face.

Tables

Incorporating mosaic tiles into tables transforms them into fully functional pieces of art. While the table remains a table—thus suitable for coffee cups, computers, or compact discs—it has another dimension, adding beauty and inspiration to its surroundings.

Tables

Tables are a mandatory feature in every house, office, restaurant, and hotel. In fact, most rooms have at least one table, whether it is for eating, holding a lamp, supporting a television, or for aesthetic reasons. Tables are often a site around which people gather, to relax, share a meal, play a board game, or work. Incorporating mosaic into these essential pieces of furniture can turn them into a source of conversation and inspiration, drawing people together to admire color, texture, shape, or size, and enhancing the atmosphere of the room.

Mosaic enhancements elevate tables to new levels. They open a full play of options and combinations, creating endless possibilities for how this basic piece of furniture can contribute to a room's atmosphere. Colorful tiles can add a playful feeling; gold or silver leaf tesserae may evoke a sense of elegance and luxury. A full mosaic surface, a scattering of mosaic tesserae, an abstract image, or a repeating pattern are all ways of incorporating mosaic into a table.

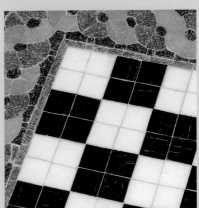

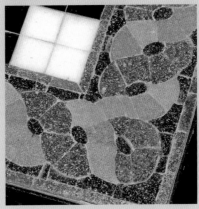

Chess Table

The table is made from black, white, and shades of green vitreous glass tesserae. The border is decorated with symmetrical interlocking pieces, a pattern that requires precise cutting and careful grinding. The process of laying the tesserae in this piece is very time-intensive. The table legs are made from black wrought iron that has been forged into a classic, elegantly round shape. The curved shape of the legs differs from the angles of the table surface, creating harmony through variation.

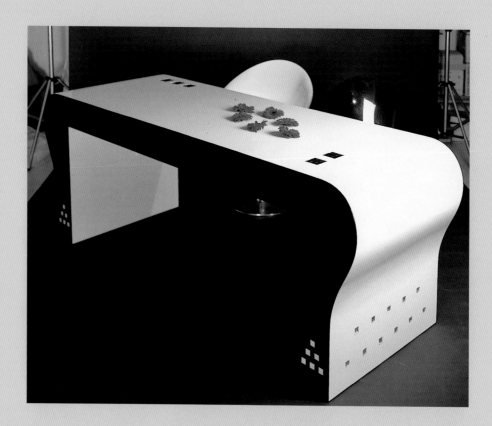

Classic Executive Desk

This elegant ivory and black table blends traditional colors with an unusual shape to create a remarkable executive desk that creates an atmosphere of elegance, influence, and good taste. It demonstrates how the placement of a few mosaic tesserae can perfectly complete a piece of furniture, just as a pair of earrings completes an evening gown.

The sharp angles of a traditional executive desk are softened into gentle, almost feminine curves. The smooth surface is embellished with dazzling pieces of silver leaf tesserae, formed by sandwiching a thin sheet of silver between two squares of glass. These pieces add brilliance to the table, elevating its inherent functionality to include luxury and elegance. The desk has a surface area of 80 by 28 inches, making it ideal for an executive or home office. The dimensions can be altered to suit a specific room or location.

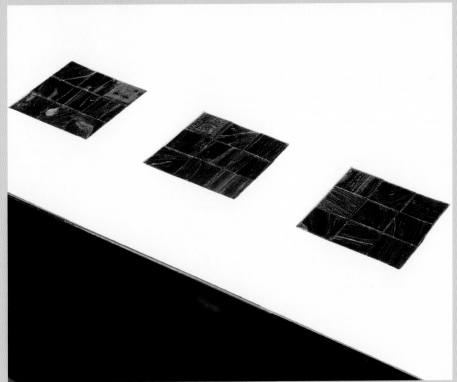

Classic Executive Desk, sectional close-ups

Flower Table on Wheels

In this lively and colorful table, ceramic tiles are used to make a lawn of grass that never needs trimming, and five bright flowers that never need watering. The table is happy, bright, and very flexible. It is inspired by Andy Warhol's Pop Art style. The use of wheels rather than standard table legs means the table can be moved easily into any corner of a room. Apply the breaks on each wheel to secure the table in place, allowing it to serve as a coffee table or end table. The table's low level makes it both intimate and practical—an ideal surface for laying CDs, a stereo, or cups of tea. It stands 11 inches high; the surface is 47 inches by 30 inches.

Woman with Tresses Garden Table

This garden table is elegant and solid, feminine and powerful. The image is
based on the mythical Medusa, but in this contemporary version, she is
beautiful and feminine, magnificent and passionate. The colors are bold and
warm, creating a sense of invitation and welcome. The table is made from
ceramic tiles, of which each piece was carefully cut and laid to fulfill the
figurative demands of the image.

Gold Flecked Coffee Tables

These dazzling and distinct tables have a wide range of uses. A single table can be situated in a bedroom; a set of ten tables can outfit a small café; several sets of tables, each in a different color, can furnish a hotel lobby or large restaurant. The surface of each table is made from a single color of vitreous glass with gold powder. The flecks of precious metal make each tile distinct, creating a remarkable play of light on the table surface. Although the tiles are all oriented in the same manner, each one has its own energy and flow, creating a sense of movement, as though the surface were always changing, depending upon the angle and intensity of the light.

Gold Flecked Coffee Tables

The table bases are made of solid oak and wenge wood. The foot of each
table is inlaid with eight tesserae, four of which are identical to the colors on
the face of the table and four of which are 24 karat gold leaf tesserae.

Walls, Carpets, and Mirrors

Mosaic enhancements transform common objects into items that are worthy of notice. Mosaic walls dress up a room; mosaic carpets enliven floors and staircases; mosaic frames draw attention to themselves, as well as to the objects they encase.

Walls, Carpets, and Mirrors

In ancient times, mosaics were limited to flat surfaces such as floors and walls. Although contemporary mosaic has expanded far beyond these parameters, flat mosaics remain an important application of the art. Working on flat surfaces gives the artist a sense of freedom and limitless possibilities; it is a solid plane that can be transformed into a multifaceted, multicolored work of art according to the artist's inspiration and impulse.

The subject for these mosaics may be anything at all. It may include words, natural or imagined objects, human or animal images. As for location, mosaics of any size may be installed in diverse locations such as subways and universities, cafés and home kitchens, swimming pools and offices. By connecting the materials in the mosaic to its location, the work becomes even more powerful, conveying through both its content and its placement the energy of its environment.

Flat mosaics may cover walls, columns, ceilings, or stairs, transforming spaces that are anonymous and functional into areas that are expressive, vibrant, and beautiful. Adding mosaic to a wall or floor is like dressing a room, outfitting it permanently in a manner that is tasteful, appropriate, and full of character. Incorporating mosaic into a frame transforms the frame from something whose primary function is to encase, into an object that, on its own, is worthy of admiration and notice. When a mirror frame is enhanced with mosaic, the mirror becomes more than an object that reflects beauty, becoming an object of beauty in itself.

Mirrors of Love

This mural is a lively, evocative collection of deliberately broken mirrors and tiles. It is perfect for a café or restaurant, or a recreation room in a private home. The mirrors create an image that changes but is always composed, a reflection of the person or object facing it. Cheerful images of hearts, flowers, lips, and butterflies create a sense of playfulness and joy. A multilingual collection of words based on the theme of love give the mirror a cosmopolitan feeling. Since love is known to break the borders of language, it is a particularly suitable theme to convey in different languages, although this technique can be used to represent any number of messages and ideas.

Swimming Pool

This project was commissioned by a homeowner who wanted a mosaic pool design that was harmonious with the color scheme of her home. Thus, although the theme of a project usually leads me to choose the colors, the opposite occurred in this case and the color of the mosaic, green, was determined in advance. With the color of the project already defined, the first idea for the subject that came to mind was leaves—naturally diverse in shape and shade, leaves evoke images of trees, forests, and natural pools of water.

Materials

Various shades of green vitreous glass

24 karat gold leaf tesserae

Nylon mesh

Plastic adhesive

Tile nippers

Directions

I sketched five leaf designs by hand, then fine-tuned the images using computer sketching. Of these designs, three were selected by the client for the mosaic.

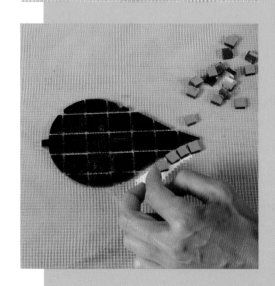

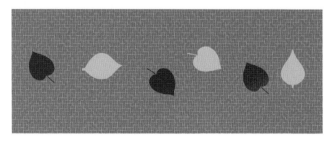

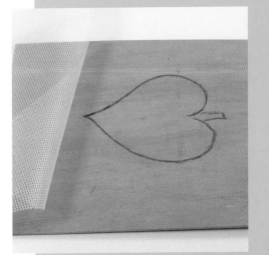

I decided to use vitreous glass for the tesserae, and three different shades of green were selected. I also chose to intersperse tiles of 24 karat gold leaf tesserae in each piece.

The leaves were assembled on nylon mesh using a plastic adhesive.

Thirty-three leaves were made in each of the three chosen designs. In total, 99 leaves were made, each one distinct due to the variety of shapes, shades, and combinations of tesserae.

The assembled leaves were brought on site and laid around the pool and stairs. On sunny days, they literally twinkle, reflecting the sunshine in diverse and wonderful ways.

Swimming Pool, sectional close-ups

72 *Walls, Carpets, and Mirrors*

Swimming Pool, sectional close-ups

Kitchen Cutlery

This mosaic, installed in a private kitchen, includes ceramic tiles and butter knives. The design is intimately connected to the room's function and the incorporation of knives (any type of cutlery would be fine) makes the mural playful and thematic. Installing mosaic in kitchens also fulfills an important practical function, as it protects the wall from dampness and moisture. The background colors are subdued, an important consideration when designing a wall that will be viewed several times a day, and for many years. The tiles are arranged in softly rounded sections that create a sense of gentle movement.

Bathroom Walls

Mosaic murals on bathroom walls are both beautiful and functional. Aesthetically, they add color, elegance, charm, and beauty. Practically, they protect the wall from dampness. Of course, frequent moisture in the room must be taken into consideration when choosing the materials used in a bathroom mosaic. The following wall designs are images that were generated by computer sketching. A winged woman, a seahorse, and seashells are all examples of creative possibilities to suit this room.

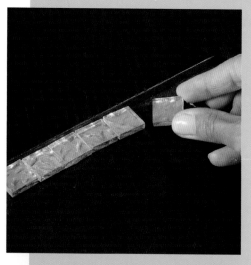

Wenge and Gold Mirror

This mirror expresses elegance, tradition, and fine taste. It is perfect for the foyer of a private home, exclusive boutique, or luxury hotel. The rectangular wood frame slopes steeply inwards from the edges toward the mirror, evocative of classic frames in a museum or art gallery. Size is a considerable factor in the effect of this piece, as it measures 60 inches by 70 inches. This magnitude enhances the presence of the mirror, increasing its sense of solidness.

Directions

The base is made from authentic wenge wood, a deep brown wood imported from West Africa. The mosaic is composed of dark brown vitreous glass with gold powder, interspersed with 24 karat gold leaf tesserae.

These photographs show the work process for the Wenge and Gold Mirror.

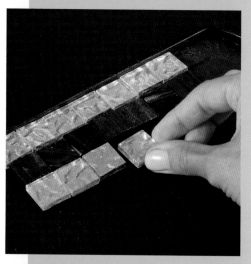

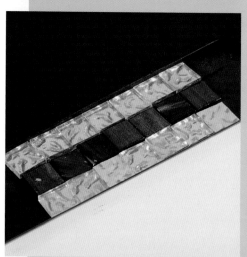

Wenge and Gold Mirror, full view

Cleopatra Mirror

This mirror features one of my favorite color combinations—turquoise and gold. In ancient times, these materials were used to create lavish jewelry for Egyptian royalty. Today, they are popular colors for jewelry, accessories, and home décor. The colors are rich, bold, and impossible to miss.

Materials

Oak wood

Turquoise vitreous glass

Plastic adhesive

Turquoise grout

Directions

The first step in this project involved determining its shape and dimensions. A rectangular shape was decided upon. As for the frame, it is 10 inches wide on all sides, leaving a reflective area in the middle.

Oak wood was chosen as the base for the mirror. An area was left for the mosaic tesserae and the rest was painted gold, and cured in a paint finishing oven.

Turquoise vitreous glass tesserae were selected and a plastic adhesive was used to affix the tiles. The adhesive was allowed to dry completely, then turquoise grout was applied, to enhance the color and provide the finishing touch to the mirror.

The mirror expresses elegance and richness, in a style that is both classic and modern, bold and tasteful. Named after one of history's boldest and most beautiful women, it creates a sense of elegance, timelessness, and beauty.

Cleopatra Mirror, sectional view

Hamsa

The five-fingered hamsa *is
believed by some to stave off the
evil eye. Each project in this
chapter features this ancient
talisman, bringing beauty and
good fortune to all.*

Hamsa

Our hands are our most basic tools. We use them to grasp, draw close, break, and repel. Our hands protect us, feed us, and help us to nurture others.

The open palm may represent various actions—it may mean stop or go away; it may be a sign of surrender or self-protection. The palm has been an important symbol for humanity since the stone age, as evidenced in ancient carvings. The *hamsa* is based on this symbol of the open palm. It is a five-fingered talisman believed by some to be a protector from the evil eye and a source of good fortune.

The name *hamsa* is based on the Semitic word for five. Some people in both Moslem and Jewish cultures consider it to be a powerful amulet. It may be worn as jewelry, hung on walls, or integrated into pictures or tapestries. It may be placed above doorways to protect buildings and private dwellings, and is a popular charm for placing in cars, on key chains, in baby carriages, and anywhere else in which good luck is desired and bad fortune is feared. Not only is the hamsa believed to be effective at staving off sickness, misfortune, and other wicked consequences of the evil eye, it is also thought to bring happiness, and blessings.

Winter Hamsa

This wall hanging features a composition of red, dark brown, and ivory colored glass tesserae laid in a solid sycamore frame. The frame is painted ivory, amplifying the power of the colors in the mosaic. The wave-like flow of the tiles is synchronized with the direction of the fingers, creating a concerted sense of movement and energy. The hamsa is symmetrical and centered in a round base measuring 30 inches in diameter. This piece hangs in an elegant restaurant. It is also perfect for a hotel lobby, office, or home.

Triple Hamsa

This striking piece contains three hamsa figures, each of which is identical in form and size, but distinct in color and composition. The combination of symmetry and diversity creates a contrast that is further highlighted by the vibrancy of the smalti tesserae against the solid dark brown background.

Materials

Wenge wood

Various colors of smalti

Plastic adhesive

Directions

The first step in this project was choosing the base material. I selected wenge wood, for its dense texture and deep color. The wood was cut into a rectangular shape measuring 70 inches by 31 inches.

Three identical hamsa figures were carved out of the wood. Each hamsa is equally distanced from the other, and from the edge of the wood base.

I chose smalti tesserae for this piece, due to their vibrancy and the diverse selection of colors. A plastic adhesive was used and applied in sections. The smalti were laid in horizontal lines that follow the natural shape of the smalti. File nippers were used to trim the smalti at the edges of each hamsa.

As for the composition of each hamsa, I had a general idea when I started laying the tiles, but chose to determine the exact arrangement as I worked. My goal was to compose the smalti in a manner that was nonrepetitive yet cohesive.

Each hamsa is based on a different palette of colors, and the position of each color was decided upon as I worked. The result is a natural flow of colors in each hamsa, and a sense of harmony among the three hamsas.

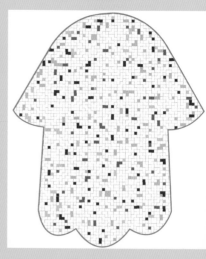

Preliminary computer sketches

Triple Hamsa, full view

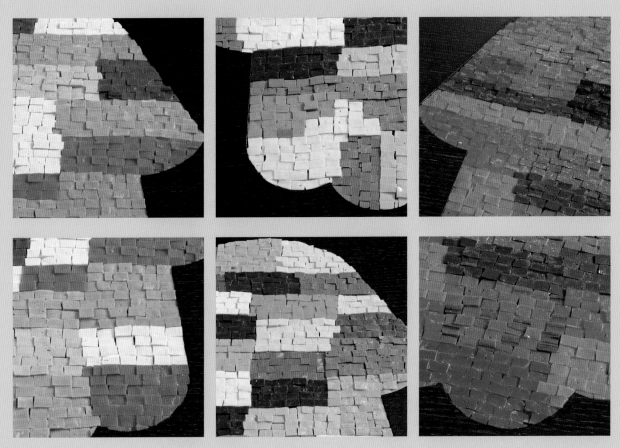

Triple Hamsa, sectional close-ups

Table of Good Fortune

This table features a symmetrical hamsa on a sycamore wood base. The base is set on a wrought iron leg, transforming the work into a functional piece of furniture. The mosaic is made from shades of green and white colored glass and mirror. The wrought iron leg contrasts texturally with the wooden base of the table, but its silver finish draws out the mirror in the mosaic, creating harmony among the diverse materials. This harmony is completed by the use of rounded shapes for the leg, leg base, and tabletop.

Directions

The steps in laying the mosaic for this table are similar to those used in the *Triple Hamsa* (see page 84). The iron leg that was added at the end transforms the piece into a table, although it can be left off to create a lovely wall hanging.

Table of Good Fortune, full view

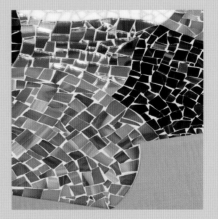

Table of Good Fortune, sectional close-ups

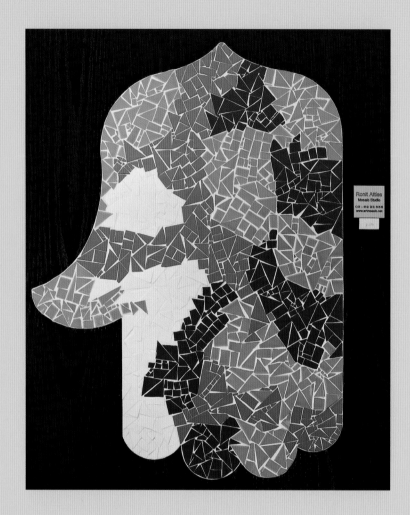

Camel and Turquoise Hamsa

This wall hanging hamsa features a single nonsymmetrical hamsa in a solid
oak base painted dark brown, reminiscent of wenge wood. The dominant
shape of the tiles is triangular; they are set in uneven, seemingly random
blocks of color. This apparent randomness contrasts with the smooth curves of
the hamsa and the clean lines of the rectangular frame. The mosaic is
comprised of turquoise, white, camel, and dark brown ceramic tiles. This
piece hangs in an elegant upscale women's boutique.

preliminary computer sketches

Special Projects

Every mosaic is unique, but the projects in this chapter are particularly distinct, due to their theme and inspiration. Some of the projects are still in progress, and computer images supply a vision of how the final pieces will appear.

Children's Mural

One of my goals is to use mosaic as a medium for helping the community. Art is an excellent form of therapy, and helping others discover their artistic abilities is one of my personal aims.

This mosaic wall is installed in the head offices of Mish'an, an organization that operates homes for the elderly and boarding schools for children from problematic homes. The wall was created in cooperation with 18 children living in the group's boarding schools.

One of the guidelines for the project was to draw a connection between the organization's two main interests. I was presented with a number of biblical proverbs and asked to choose one of them as a theme for the mural. I selected Proverb 20:29, "The glory of youth is their strength; the beauty of the aged is in their wisdom."

The proverb was explained to the children, and they were asked to draw pictures of what they understood from the sentence, and how it made them feel. All of the pictures were collected and I arranged them into a collage using computer sketching. After composing the design, I transferred it onto a large work surface. For about two months, the children and I worked together laying the ceramic tesserae. The completed piece is installed permanently in the lobby of the Mish'an head office.

The children who made the mural are delighted to show the fruits of their labor to parents, friends, and visitors. They also know that they can return in twenty or thirty years, when they have children of their own, to show what they did when they were young.

Preliminary collage of drawings

Preliminary drawings, close-ups

Children's Mural, full view

Children's Mural, sectional close-ups

Manneken Pis

This mosaic statue was made as my adieu to the city of Brussels. An entry in the 1999 exhibition at the Musée du Tram, it is a mosaic interpretation of the Manneken Pis, the most famous fountain in Brussels.

The Manneken Pis is a tiny bronze figure situated in a small laneway near the city's Grand Place. First made in 1388, the version currently on display is a bronze copy of the original, commissioned by the city in 1619. Brimming with humor, the fountain is a symbol of freedom, well-being, and *joie de vivre*. It is very popular among local inhabitants as well as tourists.

The Manneken Pis has several hundred costumes, and a personal dresser who makes sure he is outfitted properly on special occasions and ceremonies. This version provides him with a permanent costume of vivid mosaic. The front is covered in blue and yellow, the colors of the European Community; the back is yellow, red, and orange. The shell-shaped base is covered with orange, red, and yellow colored glass, and 24 karat gold leaf tesserae.

When the personal dresser saw this version of the Manneken Pis on exhibit, he was delighted and amused, saying it was one of the most interesting costumes he had ever seen.

Manneken Pis, full view, two perspectives

Theatrical Sconce Series

This series of four masks was inspired by my love of the theatre. Each mask features a different section of the face, and uses different combinations of colored glass tesserae. One of the masks also includes mirror tesserae. The masks are built on a plaster base and fitted with electrical fixtures. Thus, unlike standard masks that hide the face they cover, these masks actually illuminate, casting a gentle light on their surroundings. Both functional and beautiful, they can be installed in a hallway, living room, or lounge.

These masks were made for an exhibit at the Musées Royaux d'Art et d'Histoire. Visitors to the exhibit said the masks reminded them of the set design for a Fellini movie, or the Festival of Masks in Venice.

Theatrical Sconce Series, full view

Mosaic Bench Series

These benches are colorful and bright additions to any area where people sit to wait, eat, drink, rest, or socialize. They were designed for a commercial chain with a recognizable logo that could be modified, yet remain identifiable.

The creative process began with determining a set of colors for the series. The company itself has two colors: yellow and blue. Two more colors, fuchsia and orange, were added to the base colors, creating a festival of colors that can be used in each piece. The result is a series of benches that are unified but diverse, cohesive but distinct.

One bench is based on the shape of the company logo; others are based on different shapes, including hearts, circles, and rectangles. Again, because the company's logo is known and its colors are identifiable, the variation in shapes doesn't diminish the association between the benches and the commercial chain. By contrast, it allows one to play with the design of a well-known logo, elevating it to new levels and enhancing its strength.

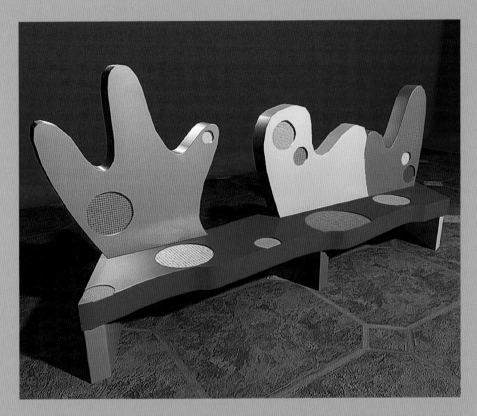

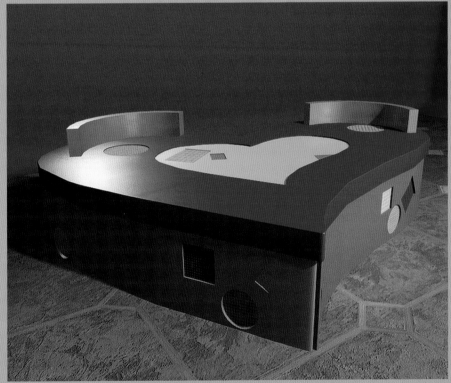

Computer Sketches

Art on the Golf Green

Playing golf is a passion for me. It is a form of leisure and therapy, an opportunity to enjoy nature and the outdoors. At the same time, golf is also a sport that requires players to concentrate deeply on self-improvement. Above all, it is an ongoing challenge in which one faces new obstacles in every game, and in which one constantly competes with oneself, striving for progress and improvement.

Because golf is so important to me, I yearned to create something in mosaic that would be linked to the golfing experience. The mosaic had to blend in with the natural surroundings of the golf course, and harmonize with the sense of peace and thoughtfulness that accompanies the sport.

The pieces in this series feature golf-themed statues that also function as benches. All of the pieces incorporate colors, shapes, and forms that are inherent to the sport. The tesserae are green, white, and gray, natural colors that blend in with the classic golf course atmosphere. The shapes are also in tune with the game. In one piece, the bench is cut in precise lines, reflecting the exactness of putting. In another piece, the rounded lines of the bench recall the shape of small lakes or bunkers. Golfers, golf balls, golf tees, and other forms are used in each piece, drawing in the main components of the sport.

This series is suited to a putting green, clubhouse, ninth hole, or any other site where golfers may sit, socialize, think, or relax. In addition to bringing art to the golf course, it also brings golf to the world of art.

Computer Sketch

Home and Office
Accessories

These items were developed to meet the demand for small mosaic pieces with the same cheerful designs and bright colors as the larger sculptures. They add atmosphere to any room, and are excellent for giving as gifts.

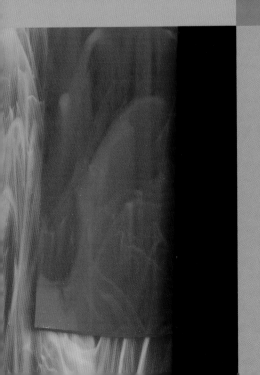

gift Statuettes

These scaled-down versions of the large flower sculptures have an important addition: a permanent marker. Designed specifically for the gift market, the back of the statuette is smooth aluminum, providing a permanent site for the gift-giver's message. This feature creates a link between the gift-giver, the artist, and the receiver. It makes the gift uniquely interactive by allowing the giver to provide the final touch for completing the piece. It also ensures that the message becomes a part of the piece forever, making the gift intimate and personalized.

While the standard height is 12 inches, 60-inch gift statuettes can be used as distinctive guest-books for large parties or important events. A large statuette with several permanent markers placed at the entrance to a wedding, bar mitzvah, communion, or large office party is an excellent way for guests to mark their greetings and blessings, providing the host with a permanent keepsake that is also a lovely addition to their décor.

Gift Statuette, full view

Candlesticks

Candlesticks are increasingly popular today as people seek to create atmosphere and ambiance in their private homes on a regular basis. These candlesticks can enhance a dining table or decorate a dresser; they may be used for romantic dinners, Friday night meals, or on holidays. Of course, lighting candles on a regular day makes the day just a little bit more special.

These aluminum candlesticks come in a variety of shapes, including sunflowers, daisies, tulips, and heart flowers. The base is smooth aluminum and the center of each flower is laid with a mosaic of colored glass tesserae. Each piece in a set is complementary rather than identical. This allows the candlesticks to be oriented in a variety of ways, either as singles or as a set. Several candlesticks along a surface makes a lovely garden of light. The candlesticks also have removable taper cups, a practical design element for easy cleaning.

Steps in the process

1 Materials

2 to 3 Nipping the tiles

4 to 5 Applying the glue

6 to 8 Placing the tesserae

9 to 10 Preparing the grout

11 to 12 Applying the grout

13 to 14 Removing excess grout

15 Final product

1

2

3

4

5

6

7

8

9

Candlesticks, three styles, full view

Flower Lamps

These bright lamps add art and light to any location. They come in five styles and with diverse finishes; each flower includes a mosaic of colored glass tesserae in its center. Depending on the style and color, the lamps may create a mood that is playful or elegant, classic or modern. The lampshade can be chosen to match or contrast with the mosaic embellishment on the face of the lamp.

Sunshine Wall Clocks

These lovely timepieces add a splash of sunshine to any room, regardless of the season or the time of day. Set with small circles of colored glass tesserae, these 16-inch clocks are inspired by the larger sunshine sculpture, Mosaic Time (see page 50). Each clock has an aluminum base, but the use of various finishes results in quite distinct appearances. A bronze finish with black glass tesserae creates an elegant, sophisticated look, perfect for an office or bank. A silver finish with multicolored glass tesserae is modern and colorful, ideal for a clothing store or café. Adding a yellow finish and incorporating colored glass tesserae gives the piece a sunny look that will brighten any kitchen or family room.

Rotating Statuettes

*These desktop statuettes have an added dimension: MOVEMENT. Each
piece contains an internal symbol—a heart, cross, Star of David, hamsa—
that is decorated on both sides with colored glass tesserae. The colors on each
side are different, creating two distinct faces. Because the symbol turns
independently of the main statuette structure, the front face can be altered
without moving the statue's base. Any symbol can be placed on the moving
area of the statuette—a company logo, personal initials, or a shape that has
particular significance. The result is a whimsical mosaic piece that can be
turned in a variety of ways, leaving the final appearance in the hands of the
individual.*

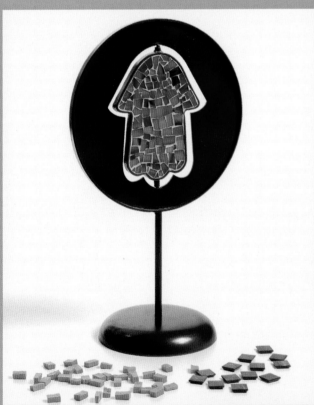

Rotating Statuettes, full view

Fashion Jewelry

Adorning oneself with mosaic jewelry is a wonderful way of integrating this ancient art form into the world of contemporary fashion. By combining leather cord, aluminum pendants, and glass tesserae, each piece is a celebration of harmony in diversity.

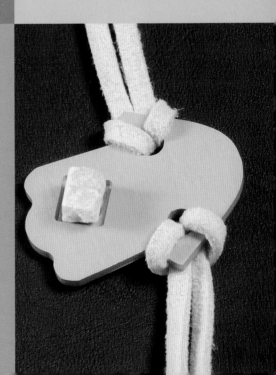

Heart-to-Heart-to-Heart necklace

This necklace features three heart pendants decorated with different colors of glass tesserae. The combination of diverse materials, including leather, aluminum, and glass, makes, the necklace truly contemporary and distinct.

Materials

Heart-shaped aluminum pendants

Various colors of colored glass

Epoxy adhesive

Grout

Natural leather cord

End caps

Directions

The first step in making this necklace involves selecting the shape of the pendants and the colors of the glass. In this case, I chose heart-shaped pendants, and red, orange, and blue glass.

The glass was cut into tiny tesserae using tile nippers. Because the mosaic pieces used to make jewelry are quite small, I generally use tweezers to grasp them.

Each piece is dipped into the epoxy adhesive and then placed on the pendant. After all the pieces are laid and the glue is thoroughly dry, I apply grout over the surface of the mosaic.

After the grout dries, I use a slightly damp cotton cloth to gently rub excess grout off the surface. I switch to an ear swab or smaller piece of cotton to remove any remaining grout.

A double strand of leather cord is threaded into each side of each pendant and secured with a lark's knot.

The chords are then tied to each other and trimmed close to the knot.

End caps are placed on either end of the necklace to support the clasp.

Steps in the process

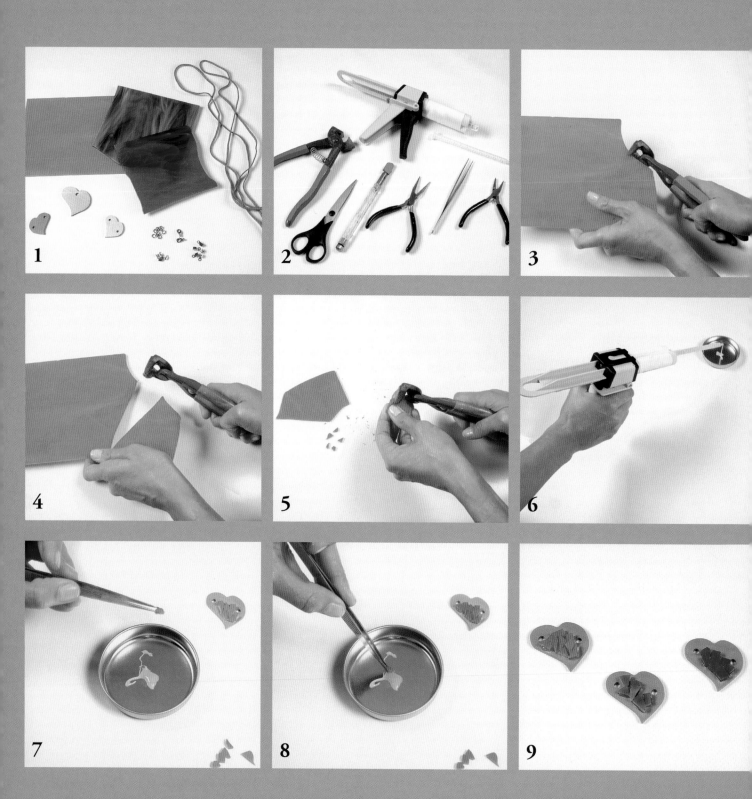

10

11

12

13

14

15

16

17

18

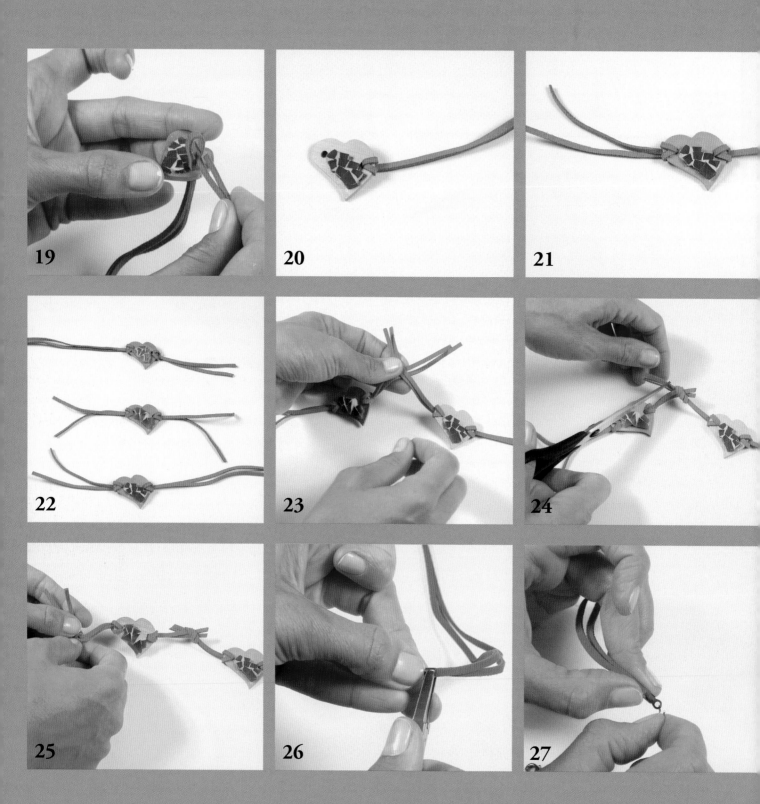

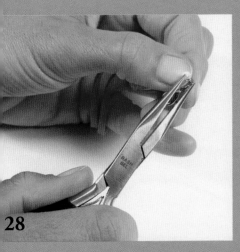

28

29

30

31

Necklaces and Bracelets

Each of the necklaces and bracelets in this series features one of six symbols:
heart, circle, flower, cross, Star of David, and hamsa.
Each piece is made from dyed leather cord, an aluminum pendant,
and glass or natural stone tesserae.

Aluminum Pendants

Index

Metric Equivalents					
inches	cm	inches	cm	inches	cm
1	2.54	11	27.94	21	53.34
2	5.08	12	30.48	22	55.88
3	7.62	13	33.02	23	58.42
4	10.16	14	35.56	24	60.96
5	12.7	15	38.1	30	76.2
6	15.24	16	40.64	36	91.44
7	17.78	17	43.18	42	106.68
8	20.32	18	45.72	48	121.92
9	22.86	19	48.26	54	137.16
10	25.4	20	50.8	60	152.4